Lunch Box Letters

Lunch Box Letters

Writing Notes of Love and Encouragement to Your Children

Carol Sperandeo & Bill Zimmerman

FIREFLY BOOKS

A FIREFLY BOOK

Published by Firefly Books Ltd. 2000

First Printing

U.S. Cataloging-in-Publication Data available.

Canadian Cataloguing in Publication Data

Sperandeo, Carol
    Lunch box letters : writing notes of love and encouragement to your children

ISBN 1-55209-526-6

1. Communication in the family. 2. Parent and child. 3. Letter writing.
I. Zimmerman, William, 1941-   . II. Title.

HQ755.85.S63   2000   646.7'8   C00-930882-2

Published in Canada in 2000 by
Firefly Books Ltd.
3680 Victoria Park Avenue
Willowdale, Ontario
Canada   M2H 3K1

Published in the United States in 2000 by
Firefly Books (U.S.) Inc.
P.O. Box 1338, Ellicott Station
Buffalo, New York 14205

Design by Interrobang Graphic Design Inc.
Printed and bound in Canada by Friesens, Altona, Manitoba

The Publisher acknowledges the financial support of the Government of Canada through the Book Publishing Industry Development Program for its publishing activities.

To my husband, Steve,
who taught me that I am everything I ever wanted to be
and who is more than I ever hoped for.
And to my son, Marcello,
who is my hero and inspiration
and my daily reminder of what is good in the world.
—C.S.

In memory of my father.
—B.Z.

Contents

introduction

This book will encourage you to connect with your children in a very meaningful way through the writing of notes and letters to them. It's something we both have done separately over the years with our own kids.

In writing such letters, you will bestow upon your child one of the most precious gifts that can be given—the recognition that she or he is loved and valued enough for a parent to take the time to write a note of affection and encouragement.

You can place these letters in your children's lunch boxes or knapsacks before they leave for school, to be opened later in the day. Such expressions of love are as necessary for the spirit as lunch is for the body. Kids can never receive enough encouragement from the people they love. Over time, you will find—as each of us did—that your children treasure these notes more than any expensive gift which you gave them.

In today's fast-paced life, lunch box letters allow you a personalized way of staying in touch with your child, even as you are separated from each other during the day—you go to work, your child to school. They are a lifeline to stay connected with your children as you compete against television and computer games for their attention. They are also an excellent way to instruct your children on your family's values.

Although we're talking here about lunch box letters, they can be given at any time—left under the pillow of a sleeping child, slipped under a bedroom door, given to celebrate a special occasion, or even posted on the refrigerator door….They can also be written and mailed by grandparents, aunts and uncles, and godparents.

As you begin your letter-writing process, you will find several sections in this book to spur you on. The next pages include the personal stories of how each of us began the writing process with our own children, and how the letters enriched our family life. One of us was doing this with her son in Canada, the other with his daughter in the United States.

To help you get started writing notes to your children, we have included sample notes to give you ideas. We have also included blank pages that you can use. These pages are bright and colorful, and some have jokes and riddles—making it even easier for you to get started. And at the end of the book is a section that helps answer some frequently asked questions about writing letters to your children. Keep a pencil and this book handy in the kitchen, so writing notes becomes a regular part of preparing lunch. You don't even need an envelope. Just fold the note in half and slip it in the lunch box.

The letters will not, of course, provide the complete answer to raising a child, but they can become one of the tools you use to help your child become a secure, caring human being. Lunch box letters helped us stay closer to and communicate with our own children. It is our hope they will do the same for you.

Why I Write

to My Daughter

I first started writing notes to my daughter, Carlota, when she began losing her baby teeth. Using shaky, squiggly script, I would write notes to her from the Tooth Fairy each time she lost a tooth.

In these letters, the Tooth Fairy would marvel at how quickly Carlota was growing up and on the beautiful tooth that she would add to her baby tooth collection. The Tooth Fairy would wish Carlota well and comment on some new achievement, such as learning how to ride a bicycle or to read. Carlota would be invited to write back to the Tooth Fairy and leave a note for her under the pillow. And, of course, I would leave some token—perhaps a coin, a beautiful stone or a fake jewel in return for the tooth.

Carlota loved these notes. And being a lot smarter than her parents, she may even have suspected a little human intervention. But she never let on.

> *Kids can never receive enough encouragement from the people they love.*

In time, as she got older and went to summer camp, I would write her notes in the "voice" and "paw-writing" of her beloved dog, Dynamite. They would be filled with humor and fun—I loved writing them because they made me place myself in the mindset of a four-footed animal and see life in a different way. Also, I knew they would make my daughter giggle. Carlota would write me from camp, and even years later from college, telling me that she longed for more letters from Dynamite.

Lunch box letters allow you a personalized way of staying in touch ...

Often, during Carlota's school days, I would write her notes early in the morning while the household was sleeping. They would include an encouraging word or two to boost her spirits on a day she might be taking a worrisome math test or making a dreaded presentation in class. Or, it might be a day when I knew I would have to work late and not be able to spend much time with her. In these letters, I would tell her how much I loved her and that I would think of her during the day. I would slip these notes into her lunch box or knapsack, or in the inside of a book she was reading for her to discover later in the day. I would try to imagine her face when she found them.

Now, so many years later, I think that in writing such notes to my daughter, I was also writing the very notes and comforting thoughts that I had deeply wanted to be expressed to me when I was a child. In writing to her, not only was I reaching out to my daughter, trying to tell her how much I loved her, but I was also reaching out to myself. My father died when I was young and had not had enough time to say such words to my brother and me.

The letters to my daughter helped me make peace with some of the pain and hurt I felt as a child, coming from a family where there were too many arguments between my parents and where there was early parental loss.

One recent Sunday morning, a week before Father's Day and the anniversary dates of my father's and brother's deaths, I found myself writing a letter from my father to my brother and me. In it I put words in my father's mouth, having him say all the things I wanted to hear before he died. His letter said he loved my brother and me, that he would always be with us in spirit, and that he was proud of what we had accomplished. What child—grown or not—doesn't need to hear this?

The writing of notes to young people, the expressing of love to another, is an act of pleasure, both for the writer and for the recipient. Every note you send a child, whether a love note or one filled with a riddle or silly story, is like laying another brick in the foundation of your child's life. It is a way of connecting. Each note conveys to your child that she or he is loved and cherished and need not feel alone, that there is someone walking in the world today who loves that child and loves strongly enough to convey those feelings in writing. None of us, child or adult, can ever be told enough that we are loved or special.

> *None of us, child or adult, can ever be told enough that we are loved or special.*

Think for a moment: How would your own life have been different if people who were important to you had taken the time to place hidden notes in your lunch bag that said, so very simply, "Dear child. I love you so much."?

Now it's your turn to write these special letters for a child in your life!

Why I Write
to My Son

The idea for writing lunch box letters to my son Marcello started simply. Marcello was about to start his first day of school, and for several weeks I had been busy preparing him for it. This was a big event for him, but as the day drew nearer I realized it was a big day for me as well. We were living on a farm in the country, and since my husband Steve worked in the city, Marcello and I pretty much spent our days together. They were wonderful days spent exploring apple orchards, walking through old pine forests, picking berries or sledding.

Now Marcello was going away for the day into a world without me.

By nature he was a chatty four year old, but on the morning of his first day of school he was quiet—just dawdling in his room. He was dressed in his new school clothes and I had his lunch box and school bag ready by the door. We had had many talks about this day and had even visited the school. But it was perfectly clear—this

> *Each note conveys to your child that she or he is loved and cherished ...*

little guy was scared. So we had a talk and it all came tumbling out. "What if the other kids don't let me play with them?" "What if I get lost going to the bathroom?" "Who's going to open my juice for me?" "When do I come back home, and why can't you come with me?"

I answered each question as best I could and told him that at three o'clock I'd be waiting with Indy, our dog, at the bus stop. I just wanted to cry. Marcello was only four! I wanted to do something to help him right then. I looked around the room for something I could put in his hand to take his mind off his worries. A little piece of home to take with him.

Now Marcello was going away for the day into a world without me.

On my desk in front of me was my writing journal, and I knew when I saw it that what I should do was write a letter. I sat down and wrote a note telling Marcello how proud I was of him. I reminded him of his teacher's name and told him I'd be there waiting at the bus stop. To give him something to look forward to, I also said that when he got home we could make his favorite foods—chicken fingers, mashed potatoes, pumpkin pie. Then I drew some silly pictures of me and the dog waiting for him after school. I tucked the note in his lunch box and zipped it up. And I said there was a surprise waiting for him with his lunch.

All the way to the bus stop he tried to guess. Now that was more like the Marcello I knew. Full of questions and bouncing up and down.

We walked down the big hill to the bus stop, the whole way playing a game about the "lunch-bag surprise." Before I knew it the bus had arrived. I tried to give him a good-bye kiss, but he squirmed out of my arms. So excited was he to get on that bus and on his way. It was a long walk back up the hill and home.

"Oh, thanks for the letter in my lunch today."

By three o'clock, as the bus pulled up, I had forgotten about the letter. I wanted to know how his day had gone. Now I was the one full of questions. Marcello took his time, enjoying the attention, and told me about his first day of school. Then, when he was emptying his lunch bag a little later, he said quietly, "Oh, thanks for the letter in my lunch today. Can we make the mashed potatoes now?"

We prepared dinner together, and he started telling me about reading the lunch letter to his new buddies at school. Some thought it was cool, and others thought it was weird. But I could tell by the way he spoke that he was proud of the whole thing. And I understood the power of that one little letter hastily written to my son. It had reassured him and kept him company in a strange new place.

From that day on, I tucked a daily letter into Marcello's lunch bag. And it became more than reassurance and company for him. It became a messenger between us. If he was having a specific problem in class that I knew about, I would include in the letter some little reminder.

Because he was proud of his letters, I knew he had respect for their content and he took to heart whatever was in them. I know that when we'd talk about certain problems he would kind of drift away—as if thinking to himself, "Oh, there goes Mama again, talking about the same old things." But somehow the letters seemed to get a lot more of his attention. That's the way it seemed to me anyway, because invariably, Marcello would come home and ask me about the contents of the lunch letter and it would start long conversations between us.

Sometimes the letters served a deeper purpose. One morning I was rushing to get my act together so Marcello wouldn't miss the bus. He was chatting away ignoring his breakfast, and I asked him to stop talking and start eating. Eventually, I shouted at him. The look on his face conveyed the depth of his hurt. It was my fault that we were rushing anyway. I took two precious minutes and wrote an apology that I packed in with his lunch. When he got home he brought up the subject, and we had a good talk about patience and how important it is to say you're sorry when you've hurt somebody's feelings.

It became a messenger between us.

Sometimes I write to him about what I'll be doing that day. When he comes home I know that he realizes I've been busy at work, too. He often asks me how this or that went.

When we moved back to the city, we got Marcello settled into his new school. Once again, the lunch box letters were a huge help in making him feel secure and comfortable in a new environment.

It took a while to get our new home organized. One morning I simply forgot to get Marcello's lunch box letter together. When I picked him up after school I was surprised to get an earful. There was a lot of pouting and a few tears. "How could you forget my letter? I looked everywhere in my bag and couldn't find it."

I was shocked by his reaction. But I was soon to make a discovery that would show me how much these letters meant to our son.

I was soon to make a discovery that would show me how much these letters meant ...

About a week later, as I was organizing Marcello's room and arranging some books on a shelf, I noticed a small white box—the kind that baby shoes come in. I opened it and was amazed to see, as neat as could be, every lunch box letter I had written to my son. The pages were a little wrinkled and smudged with pizza sauce and other stains—some were stuck together—but they were all there. I couldn't help crying at the beauty of my son who had so thoughtfully and so carefully

19

saved each one of these letters. I guess I thought he had been throwing them away along with the discarded juice containers and napkins.

And as I read through each letter I was taken back to the events that had marked so many meaningful milestones in his life and in the life of our family: all these small incidents that are so easily forgotten. Here was a day-to-day account of his life. Lessons learned and achievements accomplished. Dreams. Fears. Poetry. Apologies. I knew that all of these precious times would have been quickly forgotten, but here they all were, in a little box on my lap.

... you are doing something special by letting your kids know you're on their side.

So the lunch letters served another priceless purpose. They became our family chronicle. And Marcello was its inspiration and its keeper.

I have on several occasions been the proud recipient of my own letters from Marcello, often finding them pushed under my bedroom door or left on my desk. Sometimes they were words of encouragement, and sometimes they were words of hurt after I had punished him for something. But I knew that they were communications between us which would never have transpired had it not been for the letters.

Marcello has often come to me and asked for something specific to be included in a letter. Once when he was having bad dreams, he asked me to draw a friendly monster so he could put it up on his wall to protect him. So in his lunch letter that day, I drew a sketch and suggested we make a better one that night. He returned home full of ideas for improving our "three-headed monster guy."

It seems that when I take time each morning to make my son's lunch, I nourish his body. The lunch box letter is there to nourish his soul.

You can't be with your child every minute, and it's part of growing up for children to learn to deal with some difficulties on their own. But as a parent you are doing something special by letting your children know you're on their side. If you wonder if any of this really makes a difference or matters to a child, just think about the boxes of discarded toys barely played with, scattered here and there. Then think of what prompted my little guy to save some scraps of paper in a box, day after day.

After I found the letters I asked Marcello why he kept them. His answer? "Because I like them. They're mine."

sample letters

Dear Reader,

On the following pages you will find ideas for notes or short letters you can write to an important child in your life, even a grown child. Written notes provide a complement to all the hugs and kisses you provide.

Some of these are notes that many of us would have liked to have received while growing up, but did not. Others are modeled after notes we have sent over the years to our own children and to other young people in our lives.

Some are simple expressions of love. Some are notes of encouragement (young people need to hear that someone is in their corner and proud of them). Some are words of hope. Others express appreciation of the progress the children are making in growing up. Others are designed to help them overcome their fears and uncertainty. Some are even apologies and some are brief letters of thanks for the wonderful joy and love children give us by sharing their lives with us.

These notes are intended to get you started in writing your own personal letters. We are sure you will have a much better way of expressing what is in your heart to your own child. Use your own words—they are what your child wants to hear. Don't be intimidated by the thought of writing. Children don't need fancy words from us, or perfectly written sentences. What they need are simple words reflecting your feelings, your concerns and your values—all the things in you that make you so important to them.

Following these sample letters, you'll find some brightly colored notepaper on which to write your own lunch box letters. Some of these sheets have headings on the top or little messages on the bottom—making it easier for you to get started. (You can even include funny drawings with your letters or paste pictures or stickers.)

If this book simply inspires you to write only one heart-felt note to a child in your life, then we will count *Lunch Box Letters* a big success.

Yours sincerely,

Carol Sperandeo and Bill Zimmerman

How Much I Love You

Catch the kisses

Put your hands in the air. See if you can catch the kisses I send to you from far away.

Remember

Remember that you are special in my eyes. And when you see something that is wrong, don't forget that you know what is right.

Famous artist

In my office, I hung the beautiful drawing that you made. Everyone asks me who the famous artist is.

Famous Artist

In my office, I hung the beautiful drawing that you made. Everyone asks me who the famous artist is.

Funny circus

You make me feel like life is like a funny circus and you're the clown. You're so funny, you make me laugh. I love you for that, you silly face.

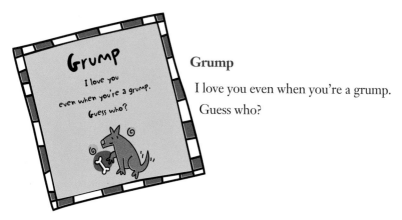

Grump

I love you even when you're a grump.

Guess who?

Hi Pumpkin

You are just so sweet. What a nice thing you did for me yesterday! I was having a bad day, and then you made me smile.

How proud

I forget to say often enough how proud I am of the way you are growing up.

Just a note

Just a note to tell you how much I love you. I think of you often during the day.

Smiling face

I'm at work now…but I see your smiling face. Your picture is on my desk. It makes me happy. I love you.

So much love

I learned from you that each of us has so much love to give someone—there are no limits. What a wonderful lesson you have taught me.

Happy Birthday

If I could borrow the moon from the sky for just one day, I'd give it to you for your birthday.

I stop whatever I'm doing

You know…I really love you. Every night after you're asleep I sit on the edge of your bed and just look and look at you. Then Papa looks too. I say, "He sure is beautiful" and Papa says, "Yes, he sure is beautiful." Lots of times, in the middle of the day, I just stop whatever I'm doing. I have to sit down and just think of you…nothing else. I guess that's why I always burn the toast!

Words of Hope

I often pray to God during the day to look after you and protect you. I can't be with you all the time, but my loving prayers can follow you. May God bless you and shine upon you.

Words of Encouragement

Do your best

I know you will do your best today, as you do each day in your life. Remember, my thoughts are always with you. I admire you so.

Better place

Whatever you do in life, try to make the world a better place. Try to be kind to people who need your help. You have much goodness in you to give others. A funny thing about goodness and love—the more you give, the more that comes back to you.

Good luck

Good luck with your test. Remember to read the instructions carefully. You may be a little worried, but I know you will do your best.

Teacher's helper

I know that you were upset yesterday because you wanted to be the teacher's helper. Everyone in your class will get a turn, and soon it will be your turn, too.

Hopes and dreams

I have so many, many hopes and dreams for you. I want you to discover all your abilities and to realize all your talents. But most of all I want you to be a good person, to reach out and help others, and to find the happiness that you are capable of achieving.

In your shoes

I put myself in your shoes. I think I know how you feel when you are frightened and alone. I remember feeling that way, too, when I was your age. So let's talk together later and share what we know. Both of us can use a hug.

Learning something new

Yes, learning something new is hard. Think about what you've already learned: like tying your shoelaces; buttoning your clothes; learning how to read, and write, and add and tell time. Those weren't easy things to learn either, but you did. So do your best.

Terrific kid

Did I ever tell you that you're a terrific kid? Sure I did. Know what? You're also a terrific actor…and you're also a terrific singer. You do so many things well. Good luck with your show and tell!

Something new

Use all of your brains for thinking today.

And all of your heart for kindness at play.

Use your beautiful eyes to see something new.

And eat all your lunch like you promised to.

Just For Fun 💡

Note from the family cat

Can't wait for you to come home today (meow) and play with me. It's pretty boring when you're not here. Nobody rubs my tummy the way you do (purr).

...and from the family dog

When you're away from home I miss you a lot (arf, arf). Dad and Mom just don't take as good care of me as you do (pant, pant!). They don't give me pieces of food from their plate the way you do. And I wish you would come home soon from summer camp. I miss my long walks with you (slobber, slobber). I miss the smell of you (sniff, sniff). I go (arf, arf) from room to room sniffing for you, but you are not there. Home is just not the same without you there to scratch my belly and rub my ears. Do you miss me a little, too (lick, lick)?

—Your humble and (sometimes) obedient dog.
P.S. Write soon (arf, arf).

Categories

I know, I know. It's raining today and you won't be able to go out to play for recess. So here's a little something to keep you busy.

Take the word **CAT**. Now think of a food that begins with each letter of that word. When you finish, think of a place that starts with each letter of that word.

(Some answers: **C**orn. **A**pple. **T**omato. **C**anada. **A**laska. **T**exas. You can pick new words and try different categories.)

I love Friday

Know why I love Friday?

Because it starts with "F" ? No! 'Cause it starts the weekend? No!

Because…Friday is movie night! Let's get a movie tonight.

Your choice!

Saturday

So tomorrow is an "S" day…Saturday!!!

Let's do some Super Stuff.

Let's do some Sensational Stuff.

Let's play

Let's play ball after school!

Fun question for the day

Here's a mind-boggling question for the day: What do you think it would be like to walk on a bridge of rainbows? Think about that! You can write or draw your thoughts here.

Something for fun

Remember that day we decided to drop our chores and do something for fun? What a great day!

You and I must remember to take another break and play a little.

What should our next adventure be? Write me.

It snowed

I loved the way it snowed those big fat snowflakes this morning! Want to go sledding after school? I'll bring hot chocolate.

Summer's coming

Hi Sweetheart! Let's see. We are now in the month of April.

So in two months it will be summer.

Remember summer?

Remember picnics?

Remember the beach?

Remember swimming?

It won't be long!

April Fool's Day Poem

Today it's cool

To be a fool

Or pretend you're a mule

But not in school

(That's the rule!)

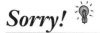

Sorry!

We rush around

I wrote this note last night to leave in your lunch box today. You see, sometimes we rush around so much in the morning to get you on the school bus, and to get me ready for work, that I forget to tell you how much I love you and how much you mean to me. Sometimes our lives seem to be rushing away from us—we never seem to have enough time.

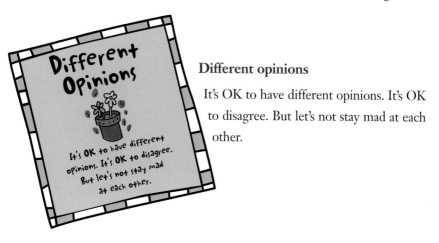

Different opinions

It's OK to have different opinions. It's OK to disagree. But let's not stay mad at each other.

I shouldn't have

I'm sorry I got upset with you this morning. I guess it was because you forgot your lunch bag and we had to go back home. I shouldn't have lost my patience. By the way, parents sometimes forget things too.

I'm sorry

Yesterday I did something wrong. I broke a promise that I made to you. I'm sorry. Something came up unexpectedly during my day. Then there wasn't time for what I promised you. But we can do it tonight if you like.

I just want you to know that I didn't forget about it, or care about it. You are very important to me.

So what about it? Tonight? Let's talk about it after school. OK?

So sorry

I am so sorry I lost my temper last night and yelled at you. There's really no excuse for yelling or losing one's temper. I was very tired from a hard day at work and just "lost" it, I guess. You know how much I love you and how much you mean to me. Maybe, in a way, it's good for you to learn that I am human and make mistakes, too.

Such a grouch

I am sorry that I've been such a grouch. I guess the pressures of work and the problems in our family recently got to me and made me forget to laugh and smile the way I really like to. When I think of you I loosen up, and the smiles come rushing to my frowning face. You bring such joy to my life. I want you to know that even with all our troubles I haven't forgotten that.

Something Special

Brand new week

Wow, a brand new week. Here is your lucky chance to have the best week of your life.

This is your big chance to:

- have fun
- do your best
- draw a great picture
- make a new friend
- learn a new word

Check the one

We've both been so busy—you with school, me with work. Let's make some time together to have fun. Please check the one you want to do the most.

- Go out for pizza
- Go to a movie
- Go to the beach
- Take a walk together
- Your suggestion? _____

Happy Tuesday!

I love Tuesdays because Tuesday sounds like "2'sday" so that means it's a day for "2"...like...2 people...like you and me. So...Tuesday is our day!

Favorite tunes

Here's a list of my Top 3 Favorite Tunes of All Time:

1_____

2_____

3_____

I challenge you to come up with a better list:

1_____

2_____

3_____

Loser has to wash the dishes tonight!

Guess What?

Guess What? Tomorrow is grocery shopping day. Would you like something special this week? Write it on the back of this letter and we'll put it on our shopping list.

37

Something new

Want to try something new? Let's pick out a new recipe from our cookbooks tonight. We can get all the ingredients and make it tomorrow night.

I can't wait

Roses are red.

Dogs like to drool.

And I can't wait.

Till you get home from school.

Keep a secret?

Can you keep a secret? Really, really keep a secret? OK. I'll share it with you. The surprise secret is…

This weekend we're having a birthday party for Michael. So don't tell anyone!

Last night

Wow! Last night I had a great dream that we went fishing on the lake. A big STORM came up and got us all wet. Then you caught a really BIG whale. Thank goodness he wasn't hungry!

Laughing out loud

The other day at the office I started laughing out loud. The people thought I was crazy. Do you know why? I remembered that funny joke you told me the other night. I'd love to hear another one.

Long week

Hi Sunshine! What a LONG week, huh? I have an idea. How about we go out tonight and do something special!

Magic wish

Why not make a magic wish today? Leave a hint or two around the house for me to find when I come home. I'll try my best to make your wish come true.

Magic Wish

Why not make a magic wish today? Leave a hint or two around the house for me to find when I come home. I'll try my best to make your wish come true.

Take a good look around

When you go outside today, take a good look around you. Look up at the sky. Close your eyes and feel the warmth of the sun on your face and feel the wind in your hair. How many different sounds do you hear?

Imagine if there was only one sound, or one smell, or one taste, or one animal in the whole world. We're pretty lucky to live in a world with so many beautiful sights and sounds and smells. And tastes.

Now *I'm* getting hungry!

Tell me about your day

When I get home tonight from work we'll sit down together and you'll tell me about your day. Maybe something funny happened that will make us laugh. Or, maybe, you learned something new that you can share with me. I'd like to get smarter too.

Thanks

Lucky stars

I thank my lucky stars that you are part of my world.

Before you were born

Even before you were born you brought hope to my heart. And the years you have been with us have brought even greater happiness to my life. I just wanted you to know that.

Good brushing

Thanks for giving Lucky a good brushing yesterday. She really enjoyed it. She says, "Thank you, have a good day, arf, arf, arf."

Good Brushing

Thanks for giving Lucky a good brushing yesterday. She really enjoyed it. She says, "Thank you, have a good day, arf, arf, arf."

I appreciate

I want you to know that I appreciate all the extra responsibilities you've been taking on at home and at school. Your help means so much to me and makes my life easier. Thanks for your help.

I really appreciated your help

Thank you for all the good things you did for me the other day. You brighten my day and make my life easier. I really appreciated your help.

Time spent together

I wish we could spend more time together, but we're both so busy! I just wanted you to know that the time we do spend together is very special.

Magical time

What a magical time it was for me to be with you when you did the Circus Movie. It was so much fun watching you hang out with the clowns and learn all your routines. Thank you for the great time.

Thanks for a great day

Thank you for insisting we go to the zoo yesterday, even though I did not want to go at first. Going with you made me realize how much fun it is to see the animals and enjoy life. I forget, sometimes, to put aside my work and worries, and play a little. You really helped me enjoy myself yesterday.

Thanks for the giggles

You have the best giggle. Your giggle reminds me of tiny little soap bubbles that get bigger and bigger as they float up higher and higher ... and then Pop! Pop! Pop!

When you giggle your eyes get so shiny and bright. They're like the sun shining off a quick-flowing stream, splashing sunbeams everywhere. Thanks for the giggles.

special notepaper

for writing your own Lunch Box Letters

The pages that follow have been specially designed to make it easy for you to begin writing lunch box letters to your children. Each page has been perforated along the inside edge and will tear cleanly out of the book.

Just select a page that is appropriate for the day, tear it out and write a note. The colorful drawings will appeal to kids of all ages and you'll find a riddle at the bottom of the page (answers on the back!) to bring a smile to their faces.

So go ahead and write your first lunch box letter right now. You and your children will be the richer for it.

Have a great day!

Riddle:
What happened when the boy mummy met the girl mummy?

Answer:
It was love at first fright.

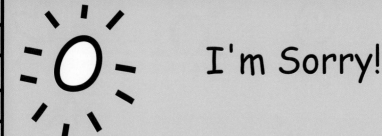

I'm Sorry!

Riddle:
The more you take away, the larger I become. What am I?

Answer: A hole.

Almost the Weekend!

Riddle:
What is the best way to catch a squirrel?

Answer:
Climb on a tree and act like a nut.

Let's Have Fun!

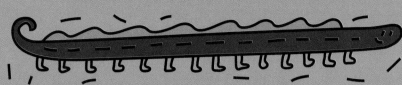

Riddle:
Is there one word that contains all the vowels?

Answer: Unquestionably.

Don't Forget!

Riddle:
What should a person know before trying to teach a dog?

Answer:
More than the dog.

Good Luck!

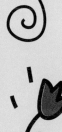

Riddle:
Which is faster, heat or cold?

Answer:
Heat. You can catch cold.

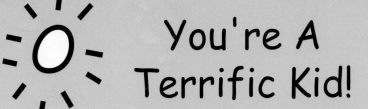

You're A Terrific Kid!

Riddle:
What sits at the bottom of the ocean and shakes?

Answer:
A nervous wreck.

Miss You!

Riddle:
What animals are weight watchers?

Answer:
Fish. They carry their scales with them
at all times.

Do Your Best!

Riddle:
How do fleas travel?

Answer:
By "itch" hiking.

Can you keep a secret?

Weird fact:
Did you know that a canary
has about 2,200 feathers?

I'm Sorry!

Riddle:
Why are fish so smart?

Answer:
Because they travel in schools.

Almost the Weekend!

Riddle:
What does a duck like to have for a snack?

Answer:
Milk and quackers.

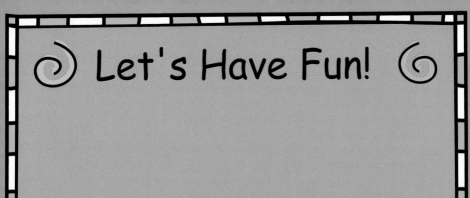

Let's Have Fun!

Riddle:
What do you call a bull
when he is sleeping?

Answer: A bulldozer.

Don't Forget!

Riddle:
How do you make a cow happy?

Answer:
Take it to the moo-vies!

Good Luck!

Riddle:
Why does Santa enjoy gardening so much?

Answer: Because he loves to ho, ho, ho!

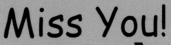

Miss You!

Riddle:
What two animals always go with you?

Answer:
Your calves.

Wow!

Riddle:
What did the elephant do when it broke its toe?

Answer:
Called a toe truck.

Can You Keep a Secret?

Riddle:
The alphabet goes from A to Z.
What animal goes from Z to A?

Answer: A zebra.

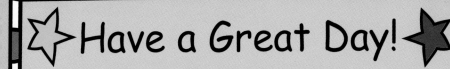
Have a Great Day!

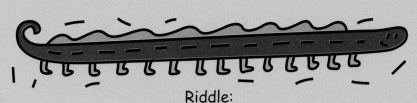

Riddle:
Why does a traffic light turn red?

Answer:
You would too if you had to change in front
of so many people.

I'm Sorry!

Riddle:
Who is bigger: Mr. Bigger or Mr. Bigger's baby?

Almost
the Weekend!

Riddle:
What goes zzub, zzub, zzub?

Answer:
A bee flying backwards.

Let's Have Fun!

Riddle:
What do you call a boomerang that doesn't work?

Answer: A stick.

Don't Forget

Riddle:
If an athlete gets athlete's foot,
what does an astronaut get?

Answer:
Missile-toe.

Good Luck!

Riddle:
Can February March?

Answer:
No. But April May.

Miss You!

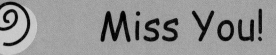

Riddle:
What does a ghost like for breakfast?

Answer:
Boo-berry pancakes.

Wow!

Riddle:
What gets wetter the more it dries?

Answer: A towel.

Do Your Best!

Riddle:
What goes up when the rain comes down?

Answer:
An umbrella.

Can You Keep a Secret?

Riddle:
What's the biggest mouse
in the world?

Answer:
A hippopotamouse.

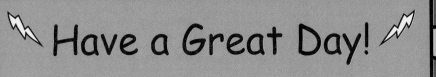
Have a Great Day!

Riddle:
What kind of music does
your father like to sing?

Answer:
Pop music.

I'm Sorry!

Knock, knock!
Who's there?
A little kid who can't reach the doorbell!

Almost the Weekend!

Knock, knock!
Who's there?
Zombies.
Zombies who?
Zombies make honey. And zombies just buzz around.

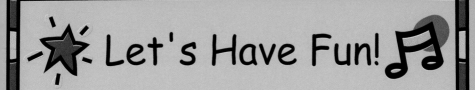

Let's Have Fun!

Did you hear about the Canadian cow who was so cold?
She only gave ice cream?

Don't Forget!

Riddle:
What kind of coat can you put on only when it's wet?

Answer: A coat of paint.

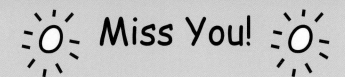# Miss You!

Riddle:
What do you get when you cross an
elephant with peanut butter?

Answer:
Either an elephant that sticks to the roof of your mouth, or peanut butter that never forgets.

Almost the Weekend!

Riddle:
Why can't two elephants go to the swimming pool at once?

Answer:
Because they have only one pair of
swimming trunks between them.

Do Your Best!

Tongue twister:
Say three times quickly: Knapsack straps.

Can You Keep a Secret?

Doctor, doctor. I think I'm a dog.
How long have you felt this way?
Since I was a puppy.

Have a Great Day!

Tongue twister:
Say three times quickly: Toy boat. Toy boat. Toy boat.

I'm Sorry!

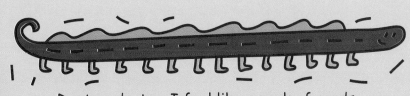

Doctor, doctor. I feel like a pack of cards.
I'll deal with you later

Almost the Weekend!

Tongue twister:
Say three times quickly:
Fat frogs flying past fast.

Let's Have Fun!

Tongue twister:
How much wood would a woodchuck chuck if a woodchuck could chuck wood? He would chuck, he would, as much as he could, and chuck as much wood as a woodchuck would if a woodchuck could chuck wood.

Don't Forget!

Riddle:
What do you get when you cross a centipede with a parrot?

 # Good Luck!

Did you hear about the dinosaur
at the rodeo?
They call him a broncosaurus.

Happy Birthday!

Happy Birthday!

Happy Birthday!

Happy Valentine's Day!!

Be My Valentine!

Happy Halloween!

Happy Halloween!

Happy Halloween!

Happy Halloween!

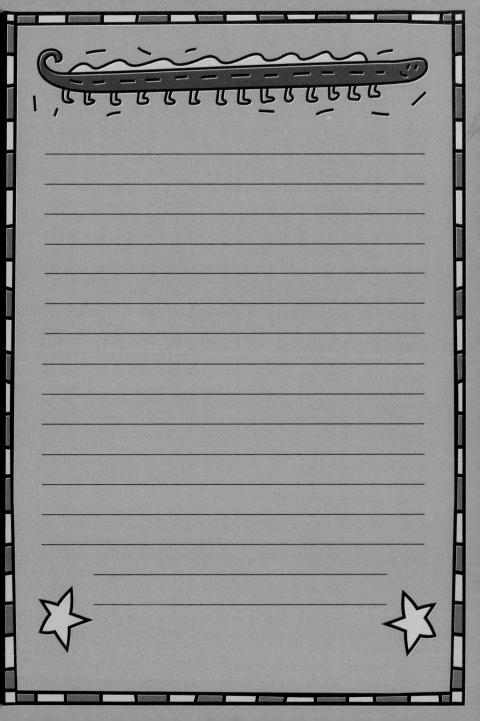

_____

_____

_____

_____

_____

_____

_____

_____

_____

_____

_____

A Note for a Milestone

_____

_____

_____

_____

_____

_____

_____

_____

_____

_____

_____

_____

_____

_____

_____

_____

_____

sample letters

For Special Occasions and Special Situations

From time to time you may wish to write a letter for a special occasion. You may also want to touch on a particular situation. Or you may want to write a letter to be opened years from now, perhaps on a milestone in your child's life. In it you can write your hopes or dreams, or share a memory or a piece of wisdom you picked up in your own life's journey.

Here are some letters we have written to get you thinking.

Hanging in there

Try not to be too discouraged by how hard school must seem at times. Believe me when I tell you all of us have found it that way. I remember having one teacher who frightened me so. For a long time I just could not "get" what she was trying to teach the class. But I kept at it, hanging in there and trying my best, until *finally* I made better progress. Do you know what I remember most from that experience? It was not what the teacher taught me. It was my ability to stick with something, no matter how hard, and not give up. This has helped me throughout life, even today. I wish the same for you, too. Don't give up on yourself. You know you always have my support.

I just don't have all the answers

As you saw yesterday, sometimes I just don't have all the answers to solving life's problems. But, you also saw me trying to come up with a solution and do the best I could in a difficult situation. I know, from experience, that by working together, and by putting our heads together, we can solve problems in our life. Sometimes we just need more time than we thought to deal with a problem. So be patient during this period. Together we'll figure things out. I need your good thinking, too.

Summer camp letter

It's too quiet at home without you. The silence reminds me of how much joy and laughter you bring to our home. I learn not to take such happiness for granted. I am glad, though, that you are in such a beautiful place, and I hope you are making some good new friends and learning new things. In the meantime, I have some great surprises for you when you return home.

Try to be patient with yourself

Try to be patient with yourself at school. Some things will come to you easily, others will take their own time and some hard work on your part. I remember the way you often have learned new things—sometimes you start out slowly and need time to build your confidence and get used to new things. But you know how with time you always gain strength and skill, and always come out in the end like a hero. Just keep plugging away, and what you need to learn will come to you. Each of us learns in our own way; some things that come easy to you are hard for me. The key is to do the best we can. Remember, I am always in your corner to cheer you on, my young hero. I believe in you.

Letter to ease loss

I know that you are as upset as I am by the loss of Grandpa. The world just seems emptier now that he is gone. Now is the time for us to love one another and be kind to each other. Most important, we need to remember that Grandpa's love lives within us, and we honor him by cherishing his memory. He is always in our hearts. I need to remember that as much as you do. He loved you so much.

Pressures at school

I know that sometimes you're not happy and that school can be difficult. But take heart. We all (yes, me, too) feel like that at times. When we feel that way, we just need to catch our breath and not think the end of the world is here. As long as you try your best—and I know you do so—you'll be all right. I really don't care if you don't become a math genius or a scientific wizard. I just want you to be what makes you happy. Tonight we'll talk about trying to break down big problems into little pieces and how, by solving each piece, one by one, we can work things out and make life a little easier and a lot more fun. We'll figure it out.

Reaching out to a teenager

I remember how hard it was to be a teenager. You're straddling two worlds—the young child you were and the young adult you're becoming. Everything is changing—your place in the world, your ideas, your body, your hopes and dreams. There are so many new questions to be answered.

I know it's hard to believe, but 100 years ago or so I was a teenager, too, driving myself and everyone else crazy. I kind of remember rebelling against everyone and everything I knew until I finally came to terms with myself. So I know something of what you're feeling, and just wanted you to know that I love you and am here for you. I want only good things for you, but I know, too, that I can't live your life for you and make everything perfect (nobody can and nothing in life is ever perfect or finished). Nonetheless, I hug you in my heart as usual. You are special and worth putting up with, even when you're so grouchy!

Hopes I Have for My Child

_____

_____

_____

_____

_____

_____

_____

_____

_____

_____

_____

_____

_____

The Letter Which I Wish Someone Had Written to Me

answers to

Some Frequently Asked Questions

Every morning is so busy with making breakfast, making lunch, getting the kids ready, getting ourselves ready. Writing lunch box letters is a great idea, you'll agree, but is there really room on our plate?

There is! In fact, these letters are important precisely because our days are so heavily packed with activities and responsibilities.

Here are some questions that we've been asked—along with suggestions that should make letter-writing a pleasure. We hope you'll see how simple and natural a thing it is to say what's in your heart.

Q. How often should I write notes to my children?

A. As often as you like. It can be as little as once or twice a month, or once a week, or even daily if the spirit moves you and you feel you have something you want to say to your child. It would be nice to write notes frequently enough so that your child can count on this expression of love and support from you. Once you start writing, you may find, as we have, that your child will start asking for notes more and more often. But, always go with your feelings—and don't force the process.

Q. Is there a way I can encourage my child to communicate back to me? Can't note-writing be a two-way proposition?

A. Hopefully, over a period of time after receiving such notes from a parent, a child may be inspired to write back. But you shouldn't pressure a child to write a letter to you. You could, however, put a P.S. at the end of a note. Leave a broken line so the child can tear off a note he or she has written to give back to you. Then ask a question, such as: What special things would you like to do this weekend? Or, What silly joke did you hear recently? I hope you'll share it with me.

Q. I have three children and I come home from work so tired. I have a hard enough time finding the energy to make dinner, much less write a different note to each of my children. What should I do?

A. There's no need to feel you have to write to each of the children at the same time and each day. Write to the child you want to on that particular day, or write to the child who seems to need some extra attention. Just try, as you always do, to remember to spread your love equally among the children over time.

Perhaps, too, you can even set up a family graffiti blackboard or white board on which you can write notes in magic marker. Use these to leave a message to the entire family at night or in the morning. Perhaps you can ask a question on this board which family members can answer individually by their own writings or drawings. This is another form of communicating.

Q. My parents never wrote notes to me and I survived. Why should I do this for my kids?

A. Wouldn't you like to know that hidden in your treasure place in your chest of drawers is a note from your mom or dad or grandparent telling you something special, special enough that you saved it all your life? Wouldn't that somehow make you richer in spirit?

It's the same for your kids. Just because no one wrote letters to you doesn't mean you can't change things for your own children and do something special for them. Each of us as parents has the chance to make life better for our children than ours was for us, and letter-writing can help here.

Writing letters opens a new door to a different type of communication. We've found that our children had an easier time saying things in a letter than face to face. I think you'll be surprised at some of the things that come out in a letter.

Q. I've never been a great writer, much less a speller. I'm embarrassed that I couldn't do a good job in writing notes to my kids.

A. Your child doesn't care if you're William Shakespeare, nor is he or she expecting *War and Peace* from you. Your child is happy just to have you and will be glad to receive a simple note that says, "I love you." Draw in a funny face or doodle, or add a flower or a beautiful sticker to the short note you write…and you have it made!

And besides, if your kids are like ours, they probably won't even notice spelling "mistakes." The thought is what counts. Your words will always be "golden" because you are golden to your child.

Q. When should I start writing notes, and how old should a child be when I stop?

A. You can write simple notes to your child as soon as he or she starts making out words in a favorite book. (You can even use the vocabulary in that book.) Even if your children can read only a few words, they'll recognize their name and the word Mom or Dad or Grandpa, and you can help them read the rest.

Also, you never stop writing notes. A child is a child is a child, no matter how old, and will always welcome a loving, encouraging note from you. Yes, our interests and needs change as we grow up, but we always welcome a thoughtful message from someone who loves us.

Q. Where do I get ideas from for the letters?

A. You can get ideas from many sources: special events going on at school, what you did the night before, things planned for the weekend. Or just write a funny poem about something ordinary like a "bad hair day."

Q. When is the best time to write the letter?

A. That's up to you, of course. Sometimes it's easier to jot down ideas while you're making lunch. Or you can write a note the night before. Many parents even prepare their children's lunches the night before.

Q. How short can the letters be?

A. They don't have to be long-winded essays. Even a quick, "Hi Sweetie, how's your day going?" Miss ya. Love Mom XO" is enough. In fact, it's quite a lot.

Q. Are there any rules about what not to include in a letter?

A. Just anything that is going on in your life can be included. Okay, maybe one rule. Avoid anything that might seem like an admonishment. Like "You didn't make your bed this morning, so no TV for a week, Mister!"

Keep it light, encouraging and sincere and make sure to follow through on any promises.

Q. My child never comments on the notes he receives. How do I know that they are meaningful to him?

A. Don't worry. Your child knows you are doing something very special. Just think of all the kids he knows who aren't receiving such notes from their parents. And, like our own kids, he's probably saving them in a special place.

To make sure he's reading them, perhaps you can add a question at the end of a letter once in a while that elicits a response, such as: Is there a special dish you'd love to eat this weekend or a movie you'd like to see?

Whether or not you get a response, remember that by writing to your children you are making a moral investment in their emotional well-being that will pay off over the long run.

additional

Hints

There are so many ways to use the lunch letters and so many different ways of putting them together. Here are some ideas:

- You can make a game of the letter by folding the corners over so they become flaps. Write questions or clues on the top of these flaps. Write the answers under the flap.
- You can tape a small gift to the letter. Perhaps: a stick of sugarless chewing gum, a dollar for spending at the dollar store after school, or a homemade "ticket" to redeem together for a favorite activity.
- Instead of drawing pictures, you could cut pictures out of magazines or old comic books. A picture sometimes helps to illustrate what you want to say in the letter.
- When your child achieves a certain goal, demonstrates responsibility at home, or shows special kindness to a friend, you could add something special to the letter.
- When your child's birthday is coming up, you could put a candle in the letter each day for several days. Let's say your daughter is going

to be six. Put a candle in the letter for six days leading up to her birthday. It's a great way to add excitement to the occasion.

- Card shops and stationery stores often feature little bags of tiny cutout heart shapes or star shapes made of glittery tinsel. Sprinkle them into a folded letter so that when your child opens the letter, a little magic pours out. This could be used to celebrate a "Happy Monday" day, or on days when you're stuck for ideas.

- A personalized crossword puzzle can be fun if you have some extra time.

- For younger kids who are not yet reading, draw a simple picture with one or two words (or the names of family members) they recognize. The idea behind lunch box letters is to let kids know you're thinking of them, so whatever you include in the letter, no matter how brief, is just right. Every child knows that XO is kisses and hugs. Fill a page with them. Perfect!

about

the Authors

CAROL SPERANDEO is a mother, an actress and a business-woman. Originally from Cornwall, Ontario, she moved to Toronto in the early eighties to study at Ryerson Theatre School. Since then she has continued to pursue her career in acting, and to keep life interesting by trying her hand at whatever inspires and moves her. Her natural curiosity has led her into many diverse fields, from fashion to farming, and it was during her stay in the country on an apple farm that she began writing *Lunch Box Letters*.

Carol lives in Toronto with her husband, Steve and their nine-year-old son Marcello.

BILL ZIMMERMAN is a father and has been a journalist for more than twenty years and is a prize-winning editor. He creates a syndicated Student Briefing Page for *Newsday*, one of the largest daily newspapers in the United States, which teaches young people about the world and which has been nominated for a Pulitzer Prize. Much of his work is aimed at encouraging youngsters to express their thoughts and feelings through writing and to engage in action that can make the world better.

His other books are: *How to Tape Instant Oral Biographies*, a family oral history guide; *A Book of Questions*, a new form of diary/journal; *Make Beliefs* and *Make Beliefs for Kids of All Ages*, books that encourage creativity; *Lifelines*, a book of comfort; *The Little Book of Joy*, an interactive book of prayer and meditation; *Dogmas* and *Cat-e-chisms*, books that communicate the wisdom to be learned from animals; *A Book of Sunshine*, which aims to remove the clouds in our lives; and *My Life: An Open Book*, which helps people write down the wisdom they have learned through their life's experiences. His latest book, *Idea Catcher for Kids*, aims to spark creativity in young writers.

He and his wife, Teodorina, are the proud parents of a daughter, Carlota, who has brought so much happiness to them.

SHARE WITH US

Dear Reader,

Please share some of your own personal experiences in writing notes to the children in your life. Perhaps we can incorporate some of them in future editions. We also welcome your comments and suggestions to make LUNCH BOX LETTERS even more useful to you. Please contact Carol Sperandeo at:

email: lunchboxletters@home.com

Please contact Bill Zimmerman at:

Guarionex Press Ltd.

201 West 77th Street

New York, NY 10024

email: WmZ@AOL.com